A Rosary for Religious and Restless Minds

The Structured Contemplative Rosary - A New Method of Contemplation within The Holy Rosary

Stephen W. Rouhana, Ph.D.

En Route Books and Media, LLC
Saint Louis, MO

En Route Books and Media, LLC
5705 Rhodes Avenue
St. Louis, MO 63109

Contact us at **contactus@enroutebooksandmedia.com**

Cover Credit: Our Lady of the Rosary giving the rosary to St. Dominic and St. Catherine of Siena in the Blessed Sacrament Chapel at Santa Sabina. Copyright 2025 Stephen W. Rouhana, Ph.D.

ISBN-13: 979-8-88870-350-2
Library of Congress Control Number: 2025934942

All rights reserved. No part of this book may be reproduced, stored in a retrieval system, or transmitted in any form, or by any means, electronic, mechanical, photocopying, or otherwise, without the prior written permission of the author.

Ecclesiastical approval for printing was granted by the Most Reverend Allen H. Vigneron, Archbishop of Detroit, 1 November 2019

Dedication

My wife, Mary,

My children, Steve & Christina, Matthew & Chelsea, and Jonathan & Elizabeth

My Grandchildren

My parents, Anna & William Rouhana

My siblings and in-laws

Acknowledgments

Any work I have ever done has benefited from the help of others. This work is no exception.

First and foremost, I thank God - Father, Son and Holy Spirit, for the inspiration that became this method and book.

I thank our Blessed Mother, Mary, for the gift of her "Yes," and the gift of her Son, for her intercession on our behalf, and for her breaking into my life when I really needed it.

For my wife Mary and my children Steve Jr, Matthew, and Jonathan, for their constant love and encouragement as I took so many classes over 10 years at Sacred Heart Major Seminary.

For Deacon Bob Ervin, my Spiritual Director from 2010 until 2018, from whom I learned so much, and whose wisdom led me to go deeper into the Rosary than I had ever imagined.

For Fr. John Riccardo, whose counsel, teaching, and friendship over many years have been invaluable in my journey of faith.

For Dr. Robert Fastiggi, a true Marian Scholar, from whom I learned so much about the human person, grace, and the mission of the Church, and for his review of this manuscript and excellent suggestions for its improvement.

For Dr. Peter Williamson, who infected me with his love of Sacred Scripture, and helped me to better understand its richness and meaning.

For Dr. John Gresham, a former Spiritual Director, for his encouragement and review of the manuscript and method.

For the faculty at Sacred Heart Major Seminary, who are second to none, and who have brought me so much deeper in my knowledge of our Faith. I hope to take what they taught me and use it in the service of our Lord and Savior, Jesus.

Table of Contents

Acknowledgments i

Chapter 1: Introduction 1

Chapter 2: My Journey with the Rosary 3
    Childhood to Adolescence 3
    College Years 4
    Trial Separation from the Blessed Mother 6
    Second Time Around 6
    Spiritual Detente 7
    Bats Save the Day 7
    Mystery Lady 11
    Spiritual Attacks 15
    A Paradigm Shift 16
    Birth of the New Method 17

Chapter 3: Method of Praying the Structured Contemplative Rosary 21
    Details of the Method 24
    Contemplation vs Meditation 28
    St. Louis de Montfort 32

Chapter 4: Bases for the Phrases Chosen 35

    GLORIOUS MYSTERIES 36
        The First and Second Glorious Mysteries 36

The Third Glorious Mystery 37
The Fourth Glorious Mystery 38
The Fifth Glorious Mystery 41

JOYFUL MYSTERIES 41

SORROWFUL MYSTERIES 43
The Second Sorrowful Mystery 43
The Third Sorrowful Mystery 44
The Fourth Sorrowful Mystery 46
The Fifth Sorrowful Mystery 46

LUMINOUS MYSTERIES 47
The First Luminous Mystery 47
The Second Luminous Mystery 48
The Third, Fourth, and Fifth Mysteries 48

Chapter 5: Some Questions and Answers about this Method 51

Chapter 6: Conclusion 55

Chapter 7: Phrase Charts and Reference/Citation Charts 57

Appendix: Portable Comprehensive Phrase Charts 99

"You Knew" 101

CHAPTER 1

INTRODUCTION

This short book aims to teach a new method for praying the Rosary that I have called "A Structured Contemplative Rosary." I have elected to use this title after considering many possibilities because it best describes what this method does. I do not use "contemplative" here in the sense of the contemplation used by the great mystics of the Catholic faith. Rather, it is used in the secular sense as an "act of considering with attention," as defined by Merriam-Webster (see detailed discussion later in the book)[1]

It is my hope that this method can reinvigorate people who have stopped praying the Rosary because they have had difficulty remaining focused while praying it. This was me for much of my life as I will discuss. I also hope that for those who regularly pray the Rosary, they will make occasional use of this method to ponder more deeply with Mary the mysteries of her life, and that of Jesus, in a structured way, that provides depth and texture that might be missed in a typical prayer session. This method is also aimed at those who have never started praying the Rosary because they do not understand that the Rosary is a prayer about Jesus through Mary. That will be patently obvious using the method.

I begin the book with a narrative that recounts how I developed this method. It essentially describes my own journey with the Holy Rosary. If that is not of interest to you, feel free to skip ahead to

---

[1] https://www.merriam-webster.com/dictionary/contemplation

the section titled "Method of Praying the Structured Contemplative Rosary." I won't take it personally. In fact, I'll never know.

I would recommend, however, making a quick stop at the section titled "Some Questions and Answers about this Method," as it may help answer some question you have about appropriate times to use the method. I strongly suggest making a longer stop at the section titled "Bases for the Phrases Chosen." Although many of the phrases come directly from Sacred Scripture, I have been very deliberate in the choice of which scripture passages I used. For those that aren't necessarily obvious, I have attempted to let the reader know what was on my mind and in my heart when I chose a particular phrase.

If you are concerned that this method will increase the time it takes to say the Rosary, don't be. Once you have used the method a few times, it should feel very natural and will add only a few minutes to a single Rosary.

I strongly recommend that you attempt to memorize the phrases used in this method. While that may seem impossible at first, if you pray the Rosary daily, before long, the phrases will begin to stick because they are all about Jesus and if you have been to Holy Mass you will have already heard them.

It's been five years since I completed this method and memorized the phrases. In that time I have prayed the Rosary every day using this method. I can attest that it is highly effective at keeping me on track, and at bringing me quickly back, if my mind does wander.

CHAPTER 2

MY JOURNEY WITH THE ROSARY

Childhood to Adolescence

My first exposure to the Rosary came when I was a very young child. I grew up in a Catholic family in the 1950s and 1960s, in Brooklyn, New York. My mother was a member of the Rosary Society at our parish, Resurrection Parish in the Marine Park neighborhood of Brooklyn. Each month, my mom would leave the house to pray the Rosary with other like-minded women. I still have a visual recollection of her standing in our living room about to leave our single family home in Brooklyn one evening. I remember asking if she was sure she was going to come back to us, so I must have been very young at the time of that memory.

As a young boy, I was faith-filled and wanted to be either a priest or an astronaut. A strange combination, but I suppose, either way my eyes were on the heavens. I was so devoted to my faith that my best friend and I would "play Mass" in our preteen and early teen years. Around that time, a new parish was started in our neighborhood, called St. Columba parish. My family began to attend Holy Mass there and I became an altar boy. Our pastor, Fr. Edward Jolly, learned of the "masses" my friend and I "celebrated" and gave us a packet of unconsecrated hosts to use, I suppose to encourage our budding vocations. When the time came for me to go to high school, I asked my parents to allow me to go to

Cathedral Preparatory High School which was the preparatory school for the seminary, but they would not let me go there.

In spite of my devotion to my faith, I didn't say the Rosary a lot as a young man. The main reason for this was that I had difficulty saying it. Not that I didn't know the prayers - the Hail Mary, Our Father, and Glory Be at its most basic level. Rather, I found that when saying the Rosary, it was very difficult for me to stay on task and to focus on what I was saying. That led to very infrequent recitations.

College Years

From 1973 to 1977, I was an undergraduate college student at Manhattan College in New York. In my junior year, I had a girlfriend with whom I fell deeply in love. One weekend, during the summer, I drove out to Atlantic Beach, where her family had a beach house. We were going to meet up and spend the day there. When I arrived, nobody was there. I waited for a while, then I found a pay phone (this was before cell phones), and I called her parents' home, but no one answered. For weeks I would call, and no one would answer. At some point, her mother finally answered the phone and told me that my girlfriend had gone away to her grandmother's and that I shouldn't call back. I was devastated. I never saw her again and to this day have no idea what happened.

Over the next few months, as I began to work through the sadness and shock, I ended up praying to the Blessed Mother for someone like her to come into my life (like Mary that is, not like my former girlfriend).

Chapter 2: My Journey with the Rosary

A few months later, my younger sister introduced me to a young Slovak woman who was very devoted to Our Lady and the Rosary. I learned to say the basic prayers in Slovak, and we would say the Rosary together from time-to-time. I ended up marrying her while I was in graduate school for physics at Rensselaer Polytechnic Institute in upstate New York. After graduation, we moved to Michigan, and I began working as a Research Scientist in the General Motors Research Laboratories.

During our time together, I learned a new way to say the Rosary. It happens that, some Catholics from Eastern Europe, state the name of the mystery of the Rosary they are praying, in between each Hail Mary and each Holy Mary. For example,

Hail Mary, full of grace, the Lord is with thee,
Blessed art thou among women and blessed is the fruit of thy womb, Jesus,

Who was scourged at the pillar,

Holy Mary, mother of God, pray for us sinners,
Now and at the hour of our death. Amen

I found this innovation to be helpful in keeping me on track. I would say the Rosary somewhat more frequently, but it was still not often. I still had problems staying focused, as my mind would often wander while trying to say the Rosary.

Trial Separation from the Blessed Mother

Unfortunately, my marriage was short-lived, and it ended with a divorce and annulment. As my marriage fell apart, my ex-wife moved back to New York with my one-year-old son. I was incredulous. How could this happen to me?! I had asked Mary for a spouse like her, and I was now a divorced Catholic with a one-year-old son living 620 miles away. May Jesus forgive me, but I became angry at His Blessed Mother for my situation. I felt betrayed and I didn't say the Rosary for a long time after that.

Second Time Around

In 1990,[2] I married my current wife, Mary (no really that is her name!) We had two sons, and we enrolled them in a wonderful Catholic grade school, called Spiritus Sanctus Academy in Ann Arbor, Michigan. This school is run by the Dominican Sisters of Mary, Mother of the Eucharist. They are a beautiful order of holy women devoted to our Lord and His Mother. They have a tradition of passing a Rosary bag around from family to family so that the students' families would learn to say the Rosary together. This was a new beginning for me, but it was still not enough to jump start a habit of saying the Rosary.

---

[2] After receiving a Declaration of Nullity from the Metropolitan Tribunal of the Archdiocese of Detroit.

Chapter 2: My Journey with the Rosary

Spiritual Detente

In 2008, I started taking classes at Sacred Heart Major Seminary, while discerning whether I had a vocation to the Permanent Diaconate. All but my first class were at the actual campus of Sacred Heart Major Seminary, which is in Detroit, about 30 minutes from my home, and around 20 minutes from Ford Motor Company's Scientific Research Labs to which I had moved from the GM Research Labs. On occasion, to pass the time in the car, I began to listen to CDs of the Rosary. I first started listening to the Rosary with Pope John Paul II in Latin. For some reason, I really enjoyed hearing the Rosary in Latin and quickly learned the prayers, so that I could join the Holy Father in the Rosary. Later, I started listening to the Rosary with Fr. John Riccardo, who was the Pastor at my parish at the time.

The old problems of staying focused on the prayers resurfaced and I often found my mind wandering to work, school, or family issues, or whatever seemed to distract me.

Bats Save the Day

Believe it or not, the West Nile Virus changed my prayer life forever. No, I didn't contract the virus. Rather, I was trying to protect my family from it. Our home has seven acres of wetlands behind it. My wife had read about the West Nile Virus and we debated ways to keep our children safe when they were playing outside. We tossed around the idea of a bug zapper, but with seven acres of wetlands, we didn't think it would be able to keep up.

Another idea was to encourage bats to reside in our woods. So, being a scientist, I started to read everything I could about bats. As it turns out, they are great at reducing the population of flying insects in an area. So, we decided to put a bat house in our backyard.

Stay with me… I have a reason for telling this story and it relates to the Rosary…

Then, on August 28, 2010 after a high school play, everything changed. As I left the theater, for some reason the lights in the parking lot were not on, so I had to walk to my car in the dark. It was summer, so I was wearing a short-sleeved polo shirt. As I walked to my car, I suddenly felt something on my left arm near the wrist like big wings. I thought, "That's a big butterfly!?" Then, I shook my arm to get the "butterfly" off and hit my car's key fob to turn on the car's headlights. What I saw, illuminated by the headlights on the pavement, was a little brown bat, and it started hopping toward me, as if it were a dragon and it was going to have me for dinner!

Well, by the Grace of God, I had just spent a month reading about bats, so I knew this was not normal behavior. I knew that bats are good flyers and echo-locate very well. So, this bat should have known that I was not a mosquito, and this bat should not have bumped into me or grabbed onto my arm. This bat should not be hopping toward me on the ground but should be trying to get away. This bat had to be rabid.

It turns out that we have done such a good job vaccinating our canine population that bats are the number one carriers of rabies in the United States. And, little known fact, rabies is 100% fatal unless you are immunized before the virus makes its way up your nervous system to your brain (the incubation period). According to the American Humane Society, this could happen anywhere from nine days to several years after you are bitten or scratched, with an average time of three to eight weeks.

The Centers for Disease Control in the US has guidelines stating that anytime you have an encounter with a bat, where you may have been scratched or bitten, you should receive the rabies vaccine and shots of immunoglobulin.[3]

Well, we caught the bat and called the Washtenaw County Humane Society. They came out within 15 minutes on a Sunday night (kudos to them!) to retrieve the bat and send it to the state lab for testing.

I had my wife drive me a quarter of a mile down the street because, again, by the Grace of God, there was a hospital right there. As I walked into St. Joseph Mercy Hospital, I noticed what looked like a very small incision on my left hand just at the base of my thumb. Little Brown Bats have extremely sharp and very small teeth and you may not be able to tell if they have bitten you, but it looked to me like I had been bitten. I explained to the triage nurse that I had just experienced a bat encounter and probable bite and requested that they begin a rabies series on me. They were quick to comply with my request.

To be protected, a person who has never been vaccinated for rabies has to get a dose of rabies vaccine and a dose of Rabies

---

[3] https://www.cdc.gov/rabies/exposure/animals/bats.html

Immunoglobulin right away, and then, additional doses of rabies vaccine on the 3rd, 7th, and 14th days after the exposure.[4]

Three days after the bat encounter, I received a call from the Washtenaw County Health Department. The person on the phone had an urgent tone to her voice as she told me that "my bat" had rabies and that I should go immediately to a clinic to start the rabies series. I thanked her and reassured the kind woman that I had already started the series.

While I was waiting for my second dose in the rabies series, I learned that they didn't have my specific vaccine. As a result, I had to wait a long time while they called for permission to give me vaccine from another batch. While I was waiting, I decided to use my smart phone to look up the vaccine, RabAvert™, on the manufacturer's website. I found a description of drug interactions that said the "protective efficacy" of the vaccine could be "diminished" in people taking Flonase (among other drugs) and that anyone in this situation should have their blood tested to be sure they are protected.

So, it turns out, that at that time, I had been on a regular course of Flonase for several years. It is a nasal steroid used to treat my mild asthma. And, since steroids can reduce the ability of the rabies series to provide protection, the only way to know if you are protected is to have a blood test performed one month after the series is given. And, for me, the blood had to be sent to the Mayo clinic for the testing. So, while rabies infections can become active

---

[4] https://www.cdc.gov/vaccines/hcp/vis/vis-statements/rabies.html

Chapter 2: My Journey with the Rosary

in nine days, **I would have to wait more than four weeks to know if I was protected by the vaccine!**

I had many sleepless nights in between my vaccines and the return of my blood test results. On one particular night during that time, I felt like I was coming down with the flu. I was experiencing chills and general malaise. **Flu-like symptoms are one of the first signs of an active rabies infection.** I woke up in the middle of the night to a racing heart and a feeling of panic. I started praying, but still became more anxious. I finally started praying to the Blessed Mother. At some point after that, I had a vision or a dream that seemed very real of Our Lady putting her arms and her mantle around me in a motherly hug. I began to calm down and was able to fall back to sleep. Finally, on October 28th (the Feast of St. Jude), I got the all-clear signal from the Mayo Clinic.

Our Lady was there for me when I really needed her. Our relationship began to heal...

Mystery Lady

After the bat episode, our relationship got another significant boost in March of 2011. I received an email from the Seminary, that on March 18th, there was going to be a meeting of the Fellowship of St. Paul (FSP) with a panel discussion on the Charism of Healing.

The FSP is a group of students, faculty, alumni, and others at Sacred Heart Major Seminary that seeks "deeper personal knowledge of God's love," and seeks to use the charisms of the

Spirit "to… effectively witness to the love of Jesus."[5] The meetings include praise and worship and a talk or panel discussion and prayer in small groups which include "the laying on of hands for an outpouring of the Holy Spirit, or for healing." I had been interested in the Gift of Healing since I was a child, so I decided to attend.

This was my first time attending a Fellowship of St. Paul meeting. There was a short talk by Dr. Peter Williamson about the Charism of Healing and two panelists spoke about their gifts of healing. Both spoke of great power that comes from Jesus and how they have used it. There was a Q&A session, and then a break, during which we were supposed to break into small groups to pray for one another.

During the break, I had been speaking with Deacon Bob Ervin, my Spiritual Director, and his daughter Karen. Deacon Bob is a wonderful man, filled with the Holy Spirit and much wisdom. He was my Spiritual Director for most of the 10 years during which I was enrolled in the Seminary. While we were speaking, another woman came up to speak to Deacon Bob. He introduced me to Ann Ward, after which, he and his daughter had to leave. By this time, Ann and I were the only people left without a small group, so we formed our own group.

Ann and I discussed the gift of healing and how I had prayed for the gift, but how I still had questions about it. She explained a little bit about the gifts of tongues and healing, and about praying over someone. She said that it sounded like I needed to pray for discernment. So, she asked me to sit in a chair while she stood

---

[5] https://mosaic.shms.edu/living-in-the-spirit/

Chapter 2: My Journey with the Rosary

behind me and put one of her hands on each of my shoulders. She started praying for me; that I would be healed physically (I had also told her I had some physical ailments), spiritually, and emotionally, and that I be given whatever I need… that whatever impediments I had to accepting God's grace be removed…

While Ann was praying, I heard her begin praying in tongues… I began praying silently to the Lord that I have the strength to open up completely to Him, and for Him to open up my heart and mind and soul and take possession of all of me. I felt a "warm chill" in my whole body. How something could be warm and cold at the same time I don't know, but that's what I felt. I have felt it before in my life at moments that were particularly spiritual. However, I was completely unprepared for what happened next.

At some point, I felt another hand on my right shoulder and another woman's voice praying in tongues. I suddenly started weeping; not deep sobs, but tears just started flowing. And, the other person, who had also put her hand on my shoulder, stopped praying in tongues and started to say in my right ear that "God has great plans for you." She said she sensed that I have many questions, but that I should open up to Him, and to pray to Him to discern His will.

Then, Ann also stopped praying in tongues and both women moved around in front of me. The second lady went on and said that God has heard my prayer and knows that I have totally given myself over to Him. She said the "He knows how you have prostrated yourself before Him and that He wants to do great things through you."

My tears got stronger…

I had been praying, for the 3 years prior to this event, a prayer acknowledging that everything I have, and everything I am comes from God, offering it all back to Him without reservation, and asking Him to allow me to be His servant, and **to do great things for Him**. In addition, for the previous six months, I had made a special effort to increase my humility by intentionally prostrating myself before the crucifix each and every day, saying the prayer *"Oh my Jesus, **I prostrate myself before Thee**, with all the angels and saints I adore Thee. I acknowledge Thee to be my Creator and my Sovereign Lord, my first beginning and my last end, and I render to Thee the homage of my being and my life, I submit myself to Thy Holy Will and I devote myself to Thy divine service, now and forevermore."* Even in the mornings when I prayed on my way to work, I made a conscious effort to pray this prayer and to at least bow my head or tell God that I am "bowing my very being" if I could not physically do it at the moment of my prayer.

There is absolutely no way this complete stranger could have known these two prayers that I had been praying (offering of myself in hope of doing great things for God and prostration before Him), because I had never seen her before, and I had never told anyone about the second prayer and only told Deacon Bob about the first prayer. I don't know if one would characterize this as the gift of prophecy or the gift of knowledge, but it completely astonished me!

The woman who added her prayer in tongues, and who prophesied to me, or had the gift of knowledge, was middle-aged and was wearing a very distinctive powder blue sweater. Later that evening, Ann started to relay the story to Dr. Williamson. He asked

Chapter 2: My Journey with the Rosary

who the other woman was, and Ann said that she had never seen the woman before but that she was wearing a blue sweater. We looked around the room, but the woman was nowhere to be found. In my mind, I could not help but associate the powder blue color of the sweater with Our Lady. It seemed to me that perhaps Mary had sent a messenger to me. This event completed the healing that had begun during the bat episode.

Spiritual Attacks

I felt called to say the Rosary more often. In March of 2012, I was getting into the habit of saying the Rosary in Latin with Pope John Paul II on my way home from the Seminary after classes. Around this time, I began to encounter spiritual attacks which consisted of blasphemous thoughts popping into my head while saying the Rosary. I discussed these with Deacon Bob. He told me that I was experiencing harassment by the devil. As I move closer to the Lord, he said, I should expect that Satan is not going to like it and the spiritual attacks should be expected. These attacks were very disturbing to me, but I resolved to continue to push on.

During our discussion, he asked if I was just saying the Rosary to check a box as if it would give me more points to get into Heaven. I answered that I didn't think that was my motivation. I really felt some prompting to say the Rosary more.

During the conversation, he also mentioned that saying the Rosary should be a time of contemplation on the mysteries of the Life of Christ and suggested that I read the Apostolic Letter of Pope

John Paul II on the Rosary.⁶ Then, over the next few weeks, I intentionally tried to think about the mysteries while I said them on my way home. That helped me to understand, probably for the first time in my life, that the Rosary is about Jesus, not about Mary. She always points to Him. I don't think this realization would have happened without the spiritual attacks causing me to discuss the Rosary with Deacon Bob. I was amazed at the way the Lord brought something so good out of the evil of spiritual attacks.

A Paradigm Shift

On October 21, 2012, I went to pick up one of my sons from a Life Teen meeting at our parish. I was about 15 minutes early, so I decided to say a Rosary (which I had been doing daily as part of a Novena for Life). It had been a long time since I had said a rosary while sitting still and not doing anything else. Most of the time I was driving.

It was dark out. I sat in my car and closed my eyes and concentrated as I said the Joyful Mysteries. I said them in Latin as I had been doing. I think that saying the Rosary in Latin makes me feel more connected to our Lord and to the Blessed Mother since it is one of the three primary languages spoken in the Holy Land at the time they lived. As I said the Rosary I felt an elevation of my being; I felt surrounded by beauty; and I felt a closeness to God. This experience is unlike any I had ever had while saying the

---

⁶ St. Pope John Paul II, Apostolic Letter, *Rosarium Virginis Mariae*, October 16, 2002.

Chapter 2: My Journey with the Rosary

Rosary, or any other prayer for that matter. My traveling Rosaries were perfunctory in comparison. I realize now that for the first time I had actually <u>prayed</u> the Rosary, rather than <u>saying</u> it. My paradigm had shifted! This experience made me want to seek to pray the Rosary more often, and especially to pray it without doing other things. I hoped to never <u>say</u> the Rosary again, but only to <u>pray</u> the Rosary.

Birth of the New Method

In the year 2000, as mentioned earlier, I left General Motors and went to work at Ford Motor Company's Scientific Research Labs. After 15 years at Ford, I retired and, as a result, my drive to the Seminary for classes from home was now longer than when I would go directly from work. Given this additional time, I began to pray the Rosary, either on my way to the Seminary or on my way home, and sometimes both ways. And I began to use the method of praying the Rosary I had learned many years earlier, but with a modification. Since I had learned that just reciting the Mystery did not help me to stay focused on the Rosary, I started reciting phrases associated with passages or events that related to the mystery I was praying that I could recall from memory. These passages were from Sacred Scripture or from Tradition, and were about Jesus' Passion and Crucifixion. I shortened the passages into memorable phrases so that I could easily incorporate them into each Hail Mary on each bead in the Sorrowful Mysteries of the Rosary. For example, for the first bead of the third Sorrowful Mystery (The Crowning with Thorns), I would pray:

Hail Mary, full of Grace, the Lord is with thee,
Blessed art thou among women, and blessed is the fruit of
  thy womb, Jesus...
...for whom they wove a crown of thorns.
Holy Mary, mother of God, pray for us sinners, now and
  at the hour of our death.

For the next bead, I would pray:

Hail Mary, full of Grace, the Lord is with thee,
Blessed art thou among women, and blessed is the fruit of
  thy womb, Jesus...
...upon whose head they pressed the crown.
Holy Mary, mother of God, pray for us sinners, now and
  at the hour of our death.

And so... I tried to think of a unique phrase for each Hail Mary of each bead in the Rosary.

By 2016, I had a phrase for each Hail Mary on each bead in the Sorrowful Mysteries completed and memorized and I started on the other Mysteries. Some of the Mysteries were so well-known to me from growing up in the faith, and from my Scripture studies at the seminary, that it was very easy to develop phrases that fit the Mystery. For example, in a very short time, I had phrases for 'The Nativity' in the Joyful Mysteries, for 'The Gift of the Eucharist' in the Luminous Mysteries, and for 'The Crowning of Mary' in the Glorious Mysteries.

Chapter 2: My Journey with the Rosary

In 2018, I started working in my mind to fill in the other Mysteries as I prayed the Rosary. In March of 2019, just before Lent began, I was prompted to put everything else I was planning to do aside. I felt that the Lord was calling me to write all of the phrases down (which were only in my mind up to that point) so that others could use them. That was the genesis of this book. Of course, I needed to finish the rest of the Mysteries which I began to do in earnest. I pledged that I would write this book by the time Lent was done.

CHAPTER 3

METHOD OF PRAYING THE STRUCTURED CONTEMPLATIVE ROSARY

We begin the Structured Contemplative Rosary in usual way, with the Apostles' Creed said on the crucifix, the Our Father on the first bead, Hail Marys on each of the next three beads (for an increase in Faith, Hope, and Charity, respectively), and the Glory Be and Fatima prayer on the last bead before the circle of beads.

At the first large bead on the circle of beads, we state the Mystery and say the Our Father. On the ten small beads that follow, we pray the Hail Mary prayer. However, in the middle of each Hail Mary prayer, we pray the phrase referring to the event in Jesus' life that coincides with the Mystery being prayed.

For example, on the **first** bead in the first <u>Glorious Mystery</u>, The Resurrection of Jesus, we would pray:

Hail Mary, full of Grace, the Lord is with thee,
Blessed art thou among women, and blessed is the fruit of thy womb Jesus,
...*whose body was laid to rest on Good Friday in a new tomb by Joseph of Arimathea.*
Holy Mary, mother of God pray for us sinners, now and at the hour of our death. Amen.

Likewise, on the **second** bead in the first Glorious Mystery, we would pray:

Hail Mary, full of Grace, the Lord is with thee,
Blessed art thou among women, and blessed is the fruit of thy womb Jesus,
…whose tomb was guarded by Pilate's order.
Holy Mary, mother of God pray for us sinners, now and at the hour of our death. Amen.

Similarly, on the fifth bead in the fifth Sorrowful Mystery, The Crucifixion and Death of Jesus, we would pray:

Hail Mary, full of Grace, the Lord is with thee,
Blessed art thou among women, and blessed is the fruit of thy womb Jesus,
…who said "Woman, behold your son" when He gave you to the Church as our Mother.
Holy Mary, mother of God pray for us sinners, now and at the hour of our death. Amen.

Remember that **in the Hail Marys, we are addressing Mary and speaking about Jesus**. That will make the passages seem to flow more naturally. Thus, it should be clear that it was Jesus who said "Woman…," and it was Mary who was given ("…gave you").

This pattern is then be repeated for all of the Hail Marys within the decades (but not for the first three Hail Marys of the Rosary).

Chapter 3: Method of Praying the Structured Contemplative Rosary

To make it easy to begin praying the Rosary in this way, I have assembled all of the phrases in chart form. I call these "Phrase Charts." In Chapter 7, I have assembled a Phrase Chart for each Mystery of the 20 Mysteries of the Rosary, one per page. On the facing page, I have placed what I call Reference & Citation Charts, which list the sources for each phrase in the corresponding position on the Phrase Charts. I have also developed a set of four Phrase Charts, each with an entire set of mysteries (e.g., The Glorious Mysteries) on a single page.

As mentioned earlier, I easily memorized the Sorrowful Mysteries, because the Passion is so familiar to me. I also memorized the phrases for all the other Mysteries and have been praying with them for the last five years. My early versions of the phrases were modified as I prayed with them to help ensure that they flow freely when praying the Rosary. The Phrase Charts have been through many drafts with an aim towards being faithful to Scripture and Tradition, while still being relatively short, and easily memorized.

I have placed PDFs of the one-page "Phrase Charts" on the En Route Books and Media website. The reader can easily access those by scanning the QR code on page 99 of this book, or by going to https://enroutebooksandmedia.com/contemplativerosary/. Having these one-page Phrase Charts in hand for the set of Mysteries you are praying should make it easier to pray using this method until you have the phrases memorized.

Details of the Method

While developing this Structured Contemplative Rosary, I have invoked the Holy Spirit to enlighten me along the way and to help me choose the right phrases. I hope the final product is a result of that requested "collaboration." For sure, anything good about this work is His, and anything less well done is due to my human failings getting in the way.

The phrases I have selected are of course not the only ones that could have been chosen. Most of the phrases I have included are obvious, coming directly from Sacred Scripture or the Tradition of the Church. For some, I had to do a little extra research or give some more thought.

As I began to write this book, I began to feel a lot of doubt and trepidation. I believe that these were spiritual attacks. Things like "Would anyone else find this way of praying the Rosary helpful?" and "Is what I am doing sacrilegious?" among other doubts, surfaced in my mind. Once I identified those as spiritual attacks, I became all the more determined to write this book and get this method out to as many people as might benefit from it.

Back in 2012, at my Spiritual Director, Deacon Bob's suggestion, I <u>did</u> read the Apostolic Letter of St. Pope John Paul II [7], "On the Most Holy Rosary." In this letter, the Pope explained that praying the Rosary leads us to "[sit] at the school of Mary" where we "contemplate the beauty of the face of Christ and

---

[7] St. Pope John Paul II, Apostolic Letter, *Rosarium Virginis Mariae*, October 16, 2002.

experience the depth of His love." [8] He also said that the Rosary is "Marvelous in its simplicity and its depth." This is one source of my anxiety. The Rosary as traditionally said is composed of four prayers learned from the youngest ages for most Catholics. My sixth grade Catechism students knew the Hail Mary, Our Father, and Glory Be, and I expect that some of them knew the Apostles Creed by heart (although I never asked them about it). This simplicity allows the Rosary to be prayed anywhere and anytime, and to be prayed communally by any group of reasonably well-formed Catholics.

In contrast, the method I am proposing does not at first seem simple. While it is my belief that the true power of this method will be best experienced if the phrases are memorized, for sure, it will require many repetitions of the Rosary to learn/remember all the phrases I have compiled. Yet, they are from very familiar Scripture passages and Church Tradition, and they are historical events as outlined in the Gospels and Epistles. Therefore, they should be reasonably memorable. In addition, I have striven to keep the phrases short to facilitate their memorization. Certainly, in my own experience, very early on I memorized all of the phrases for the Sorrowful Mysteries without much problem and could pray those anywhere and anytime. Since writing this book, this method is the only way I pray the Rosary, and since I pray it daily, I have all 200 phrases memorized.

---

[8] St. Pope John Paul II, Apostolic Letter, *Rosarium Virginis Mariae*, October 16, 2002, Section 2.

That said, memorization is not required. As mentioned earlier, I have put together charts of the phrases which make it very easy to pray the Rosary if you are willing to hold a piece of paper in your hand as you pray. In fact, all of the phrases for a single set of mysteries, e.g., The Joyful Mysteries, can fit on a single 8-1/2 by 11-inch piece of paper. So, anyone who can read can just use the Phrase Charts and be praying this Structured Contemplative Rosary immediately (see the Appendix for the four Phrase Charts).

In his Apostolic Letter, the Holy Father said that "the most important reason for strongly encouraging the practice of the Rosary is that it represents a most effective means of fostering among the faithful that commitment to contemplation of the Christian mystery." [9] Using the proposed method, these phrases have certainly helped me to more fully recall the events in the life of Christ so as to more fully appreciate and "experience the depth of His love."

Still, over and over in the letter, the Holy Father refers to using the Rosary as a tool for meditation and contemplation that calls for "a quiet rhythm and a lingering pace." That came through in the following excerpts from the Holy Father's letter:

> "To recite the Rosary is nothing other than to <u>contemplate</u> with Mary the face of Christ." – Section 3
>
> "The Rosary belongs among the finest and most praiseworthy traditions of Christian <u>contemplation</u>." – Section 5

---

[9] St. Pope John Paul II, Apostolic Letter, *Rosarium Virginis Mariae*, October 16, 2002, Section 5.

Chapter 3: Method of Praying the Structured Contemplative Rosary

"Mary constantly sets before the faithful the 'mysteries' of her Son, with the desire that the <u>contemplation</u> of those mysteries will release all their saving power." – Section 11

"The Rosary, precisely because it starts with Mary's own experience is an exquisitely <u>contemplative</u> prayer." – Section 12

"Without <u>contemplation</u>, the Rosary is a body without a soul, and its repetition runs the risk of becoming a mechanical repetition of formulas…" Section 12

"The Rosary is both <u>meditation</u> and supplication." – Section 16

"The Rosary is one of the traditional paths of Christian prayer directed to the <u>contemplation</u> of Christ's face." – Section 18

"…the succession of Hail Marys constitutes the warp on which is woven the <u>contemplation</u> of the mysteries." – Section 18

"The cycles of <u>meditation</u> proposed by the Holy Rosary are by no means exhaustive, but they do bring to mind what is essential, and they awaken in the soul a thirst for a knowledge of Christ continually nourished by the pure source of the Gospel." – Section 23

"Anyone who <u>contemplates</u> Christ through the various stages of His life cannot fail to perceive in Him the truth about man." – Section 25

"<u>Meditation</u> on the mysteries of Christ is proposed in the Rosary by means of a method designed to assist in their assimilation. It is a method based on repetition. This applies above all to the Hail Mary, repeated ten times in each mystery. If this repetition is considered superficially, there could be a temptation to see the Rosary as a dry and boring exercise. It is quite another thing, however, when the Rosary is thought of as an outpouring of that love which tirelessly returns to the person loved with expressions similar in their content but ever fresh in terms of the feeling pervading them." – Section 26

Contemplation vs Meditation

Given all this talk of contemplation and meditation by the Holy Father, I was concerned that this new method would eliminate the ability to experience contemplation. So, I undertook a review of the differences between meditation and contemplation.

Contemplation is defined by Merriam-Webster[10] as:

> 1a: concentration on spiritual things as a form of private devotion
> 1b: a state of mystical awareness of God's being
> **2: an act of considering with attention**
> 3: the act of regarding steadily

On the other hand, **Meditation** is defined by Merriam-Webster[11] as:

> 1: a discourse intended to express its author's reflections or to guide others in contemplation
> 2: the act or process of meditating

And **Meditate** is defined by Merriam-Webster[12] as:

---

[10] https://www.merriam-webster.com/dictionary/contemplation
[11] https://www.merriam-webster.com/dictionary/meditation

Chapter 3: Method of Praying the Structured Contemplative Rosary

1: to engage in contemplation or reflection

2: to engage in mental exercise (such as concentration on one's breathing or repetition of a mantra) for the purpose of reaching a heightened level of spiritual awareness

Given these definitions (which appear to be somewhat circular to me), an argument can be made that this so-called "Structured Contemplative" method can indeed be considered contemplative. I believe this is true in the secular sense of the word (definition 2), unlike contemplation in the spiritual sense (definition 1b) which involves trying to place oneself in the presence of God to communicate on a spiritual level.

There are several other statements, made by the Holy Father in the Apostolic Letter, which also helped relieve my anxiety relative to this method of praying the Rosary. For example, in Section 13, the Holy Father notes that "Mary's contemplation is above all a remembering... [that makes] present... the works brought about by God in the history of salvation." While it may not lead to "spiritual contemplation," this method does elicit a remembering of the events in Mary's and Jesus' lives by its very nature or definition.

Similarly, I am most heartened by the Holy Father's headings for Sections 27 and 28 which are:

"A valid method..." (Heading for Section 27), "...which can nevertheless be improved" (Heading for Section 28)

---

[12] https://www.merriam-webster.com/dictionary/meditate

The Holy Father notes that God communicates Himself to us, "respecting our human nature and its vital rhythms." [13] In fact, theologians call this the Incarnational Principle.[14] That principle explains how, since man is sensory in being (i.e., we experience our world with the use of our physical senses of sight, hearing, taste, smell, and touch), God uses instruments that exist in space and time that can be perceived by those senses to communicate and interact with humans.

Meditation, as in the repetition of a mantra (e.g., the Hail Mary in the case of the Rosary), is "linked to the rhythm of breathing". He notes that in the West, there is a "renewed demand for meditation," and that "the Rosary is simply a method of contemplation." [15] Importantly, the Holy Father warns that the method is "a means to an end and cannot become an end in itself."

The next section of the Apostolic Letter, in fact, the entire substance of Chapter 3 in the letter, deals with different ways to pray the Rosary.[16] These include, announcing each mystery with a suitable icon or image to help the participants have a visual image that can stimulate the imagination (as in the method of prayer of St. Ignatius of Loyola). Another method is to read a Biblical

---

[13] St. Pope John Paul II, Apostolic Letter, *Rosarium Virginis Mariae*, October 16, 2002, Section 27.

[14] Stephen B. Clark, *Catholics and the Eucharist: A Scriptural Introduction*, Servant Publications, Ann Arbor, MI, page 22, 2000.

[15] St. Pope John Paul II, Apostolic Letter, *Rosarium Virginis Mariae*, October 16, 2002, Section 28.

[16] St. Pope John Paul II, Apostolic Letter, *Rosarium Virginis Mariae*, October 16, 2002, Section 29.

passage to provide "foundation and depth to [the] meditation." [17] The Holy Father seemed pleased to include the word of God as found in Sacred Scripture and saw it as a way to pray the Rosary without "giving rise to the ennui derived from simpler recollection of something already well-known." It is apparent that the Holy Father envisioned the announcement of the mystery and the proclamation of the word of God as preceding the start of the Hail Marys, because he called for a period of silence before the vocal prayer begins to allow time for the mystery to soak in.

Interestingly, the Holy Father appears to mention the method of praying the Rosary that I learned from the Slovak faithful I knew earlier in my life. He notes that Pope Paul VI wrote in his Apostolic Exhortation, *Marialis Cultus*, that in some regions, the faithful add the name of Jesus and a reference to the mystery being contemplated with each Hail Mary.[18] The Holy Father, calls this "a praiseworthy custom." Further, he says "It is at once a profession of faith and an aid in concentrating on our meditation since it facilitates the process of assimilation to the mystery of Christ inherent in the repetition of the Hail Mary." [19]

Finally for our purposes, after explaining the new Luminous Mysteries of the Holy Rosary in his letter, the Holy Father expresses the hope that they will be widely circulated and used

---

[17] St. Pope John Paul II, Apostolic Letter, *Rosarium Virginis Mariae*, October 16, 2002, Section 30.

[18] St. Pope Paul VI, Apostolic Exhortation, *Marialis Cultus*, February 2, 1974, Section 46.

[19] St. Pope John Paul II, Apostolic Letter, *Rosarium Virginis Mariae*, October 16, 2002, Section 33.

experimentally "…in centers and shrines particularly devoted to the Rosary, so that the people of God may benefit from an abundance of authentic spiritual riches and find nourishment for their personal contemplation." [20] It is my hope that the same will be done with this Structured Contemplative Rosary.

St. Louis de Montfort

One morning, just after Lent began this year (2020), I was looking for something spiritually enriching to read. I found a book[21] called "The Secrets of the Rosary" by St. Louis de Monfort and picked it up to read it. It had been sent to me sometime in the recent past by an organization called "America Needs Fatima," which is a wonderful organization that promotes devotion to Our Lady, in general, and especially to Our Lady of Fatima.

As I perused the book, I noticed that just as Saint Pope John Paul II listed different ways to pray the Rosary in his Apostolic Letter, St. Louis de Montfort included five methods for praying the Rosary in "Part II" of his book. The second method proposed by St. Louis is very much like the method I learned from the Slovak faithful. The third method, however, is essentially the same, in principle, as the method I propose in this work. The main difference is that, whereas St. Louis de Montfort uses full sentences

---

[20] St. Pope John Paul II, Apostolic Letter, *Rosarium Virginis Mariae*, October 16, 2002, Section 35.

[21] St. Louis de Montfort, *The Secret of the Rosary*, from America Needs Fatima, Hanover, PA.

Chapter 3: Method of Praying the Structured Contemplative Rosary

meant to elicit thoughtful meditation, I have chosen very short phrases in order to help recall specific events in the life of Christ.

The meditations suggested by St. Louis are not easily obtained and require deep thought and significant use of one's imagination. These comments are not meant in a disparaging way, rather just to point out that much more concentration is required using St. Louis' method. Such a level of thought would be very useful in eliciting deep contemplation and with enough time to dwell with Our Lady and Jesus in the Rosary.

For the average person, today's world is nearly devoid of time to dwell on anything. We are all too busy and in seemingly perpetual motion, both physically and mentally. The premise of this work is that for someone without as much time, and with a lot on their restless mind, a less demanding set of contemplations could be helpful. The method I have proposed allows one to connect with Jesus and Mary using mainly familiar phrases from Scripture and Tradition of the Church which should not require such deep thought. They do not preclude one getting lost in the Rosary when time permits and may also facilitate that. But they also do not require one to have a lot of time for deep contemplation.

In addition, the phrases I have chosen always flow continuously from the Hail Mary prayer. They always relate to something specific within the Mystery being prayed and are either about Jesus, about Mary, or about both of them. While St. Louis clearly had the idea for a contemplative Rosary more than 300 years before I did, I believe the difference between our implementations will make it much easier for the modern mind to use the method I propose. In fact, in the five years since I completed this method, I have used it to pray the Rosary every day and have found it to be extremely effective at keeping me focused and bringing me back if my mind does stray.

CHAPTER 4

BASES FOR THE PHRASES CHOSEN

As noted earlier, I have compiled a "Phrase Chart" for each set of Mysteries which gives the phrases I selected for use while praying. For each set of Mysteries there is a corresponding "Reference & Citation Chart" showing the basis for the phrase whether from Sacred Scripture or elsewhere. These charts can be found in Chapter 7 ("PHRASE CHARTS AND REFERENCE /CITATION CHARTS").

Most of the phrases used in this Structured Contemplative Rosary are either direct quotes from Sacred Scripture or have been adapted directly from it. Some of the phrases are reflections of the Tradition of the Church or from Papal documents. Still others, fewer in number are the product of some research on my part, of published works, to fill in gaps of knowledge not contained in Scripture or Tradition. For example, in the Sorrowful Mysteries, very few of the phrases for "The Scourging at the Pillar" mystery are from Scripture, because there is no description of scourging in Sacred Scripture. Everyone in Jesus' time knew what it meant to be scourged. So, I consulted other sources from historical and medical scholarly journals to fill in the gaps. I will mostly discuss the anomalies in the following. That is, those phrases not purely from Sacred Scripture. In a few other instances, I will explain the reasons I have used a specific passage from Sacred Scripture.

In addition, I have taken phrases from Sacred Scripture without regard to potentially conflicting passages. For example, I have taken phrases about the coming of the Holy Spirit from both the Synoptic Gospels (Matthew, Mark and Luke) and from John's Gospel which give different accounts. I have not tried to reconcile differences or favor one over the other. Although I do try to explain my reasoning for using the phrases chosen, I simply used what I believe will be memorable and is Scriptural.

In several of the Mysteries, I used parallel construction with the first phrase and last phrase. Likewise, in several of the Mysteries, the fifth phrase was intentionally the culmination of the Mystery. Both of these literary techniques were done to aid in memorization. I was only able to accomplish this for a few of the Mysteries, but in any event believe that it will help with memorization.

For many of the Mysteries, I tried to incorporate important and/or well-known concepts from Sacred Scripture and Tradition. I will point them out in the pages that follow.

GLORIOUS MYSTERIES

The First and Second Glorious Mysteries

The first two mysteries contain phrases, entirely derived from Sacred Scripture, which obviously relate to or describe the mysteries, so no explanation is required for those.

However, a note about the choice of one phrase I used in the Resurrection Mystery is warranted. In Matthew's Gospel (Mt 28:2)

Chapter 4: Bases for the Phrases Chosen

an Angel rolls away the stone from Jesus's tomb, but in the three other Gospels the stone had already been rolled away when Mary Magdalene arrived. Rather than choose between the Gospels, I deliberately made the phrase ambiguous. That is, to say, the phrase "…whose tombstone was rolled away when Mary Magdalene arrived," could mean the actual action of rolling the stone away <u>occurred when Mary arrived</u>; but it could also mean that the tombstone was <u>already</u> rolled away when Mary arrived. So, no choice between the Gospels was needed.

I intentionally chose the "Divine Commission" as the fourth phrase in the Mystery of the Ascension as a reminder to all of us that this command was not just for the Apostles but for every baptized Christian.

The Third Glorious Mystery

While the phrases used for the Mystery describing the Gift of the Holy Spirit are also all taken from Sacred Scripture, a bit of explanation is useful here too. In Chapter 20 of St. John's Gospel, as mentioned, John gives an account of the Apostles reception of the Holy Spirit which is different from the account given by St. Luke in Chapter 2 of Acts of the Apostles. I have made no attempt to reconcile the two accounts but have provided phrases from both accounts in chronological order, recalling that St. John's account was on Easter evening and the account in Acts was on Pentecost, fifty days later.

Some commentaries suggest that St. John's account refers to Jesus preparing the Apostles for reception of the Spirit on

Pentecost. I don't believe this suggestion is necessary to assume. Throughout Acts, the Holy Spirit falls on different groups at different times. In John's Gospel, Thomas was not present when Jesus breathed on the disciples. In Acts 2, the Apostles were present along with Mary, the mother of Jesus, and some other disciples and women. Therefore, these accounts do not necessarily reflect inconsistency. Rather, they reflect two instances of the descent of the Holy Spirit, with the one in Acts 2, recording a much more dramatic result. The different result may be because it was the right time for Peter to begin his career as an evangelist, as the shock of the Resurrection had worn off, and its implications were becoming apparent to the Apostles.

The Fourth Glorious Mystery

The Assumption of Mary into Heaven, is not explicitly mentioned in Sacred Scripture, but is entirely consistent with Sacred Scripture. As the Church Fathers have shown, this mystery, handed down in the Tradition of the Church from its earliest days, finds support in various Scriptures when understood in their fuller sense.[22] After reading many of the Church documents on the Assumption, I chose phrases that I thought would best demonstrate how the only logical outcome for the Blessed Mother of Jesus at the end of her life would be the Assumption. When one considers:

---

[22] St. Pope John Paul II, General Audience, July 2, 1997, Section 2.

Chapter 4: Bases for the Phrases Chosen

- that Mary was conceived without Original Sin (a prerequisite for containing God within her womb because it is inconceivable that God would become incarnate in the womb of a mother who had once been under the domain of sin),
- that God the Father asked Mary to bear His Son,
- that Mary said yes, at great personal cost,
- that Mary bore Jesus within her womb, gave birth to Him, nourished Him, raised Him, undoubtedly taught Him how to pray, and helped to keep Him safe throughout His life,
- that Mary was the first disciple of Jesus,[23]
- and that Mary accompanied Jesus through His whole life, Passion, and death, without ever leaving Him, even while He was on the Cross, and
- the love that a Son has for His Mother, especially Jesus for Mary,

then, it makes total sense that Jesus would not want Mary's body to undergo decay, and would want to honor His mother at the end of her life on earth. The phrases build this argument to its logical conclusion "…who took you up into Heaven at the end of your life on earth."

That God had chosen to "assume" other people in salvation history gives even more rationale for Jesus taking His Blessed Mother up at the end of her life. After all in Genesis 5:22-24, we

---

[23] St. Pope John Paul II, *Redemptoris Mater*, 3/25/1987, No 26, Paragraph 5.

learn the God took Enoch into heaven, and in 2 Kings 2:11, God takes Elijah up to heaven. While these were undoubtedly holy men, neither could compare to our Blessed Mother in their cooperation in the cause our redemption.

The last phrase in the Mystery of the Assumption is another that has been deliberately made somewhat ambiguous. The reason for this is that the Pope and Magisterium of the Church have never issued a definitive statement as to whether Mary died and was taken up into Heaven or was taken up before she died. In a general audience on July 2, 1997, then Pope John Paul II, noted that Pius XII "did not take a position on the question of the Blessed Virgin's death as a truth of faith." [24] While it is clear from the text of the audience that Pope John Paul II believed Mary had died, he did not state it as a matter of doctrine. So, I've written this phrase in a way that it could mean Mary had already died when she was taken up into Heaven, or that just before she would have died, she was taken up. Both meanings would be in keeping with the faith.

The documents used to develop the basis for these phrases consisted of those listed on the Reference Charts, including, in chronological order, the Council of Ephesus in 431 AD (in Neuner and Depuis #605 and #701), Constitution *Cum Praexcelsa* by Pope Sixtus IV in 1477 (in Neuner and Depuis #704), the Council of Trent in 1546 (in Neuner and Depuis #705), Ineffabilis Deus (1854), Munificentissimus Deus (1950), Lumen Gentium (1964), and Redemptoris Mater (1987).

---

[24] St. Pope John Paul II, General Audience, July 2, 1997, Section 2.

Chapter 4: Bases for the Phrases Chosen

The Fifth Glorious Mystery

The Crowning of Mary, Queen of Heaven and Earth, is another mystery that is not explicitly mentioned in Scripture. Nevertheless, Church Tradition has given this Mystery its substance. That Mary is Queen of Heaven and Earth is gleaned from the Apostolic Constitution of Pope Pius XII, called Munificentissimus Deus (1950). The rest of the phrases for this Mystery come entirely from the Litany of Loreto, which was promulgated by Pope Sixtus V in 1587, and which had additional titles added throughout the centuries following. To aid in memorization, the titles representing Mary as Queen over a specific group of persons are in alphabetical order. Note the definite article "the" is used in front of Apostles and Patriarchs because we know who they were. In comparison, there are many angels, martyrs and saints about whom we have no knowledge, so the implication is that Mary is Queen of all of them.

Finally, the phrase used after the seventh Hail Mary in the Crowning of Mary Mystery is one that I consider to be an optional phrase. I have included other phrases below the table that could be used for particular devotions such as Our Lady of Fatima, Our Lady of Good Counsel, etc. You can replace that with a different title for Mary from the Litany of Loreto that you prefer.

JOYFUL MYSTERIES

The phrases for the Joyful Mysteries are all direct quotes or derived directly from Sacred Scripture, and therefore, need no explanations. However, there is one exception, and that is the third phrase in the Nativity Mystery. This phrase, "…who was born in a cave," while not in Sacred Scripture, represents Church Tradition as acknowledged in a statement made by St. Justin Martyr in the Dialogue with Trypho,[25] around the year 155 AD. St. Justin said:

> *"But when the Child was born in Bethlehem, since Joseph could not find a lodging in that village, **he took up his quarters in a certain cave** near the village; and while they were there Mary brought forth the Christ and placed Him in a manger, and here the Magi who came from Arabia found Him."*

While it is clearly directly from sacred Scripture, there was no question in my mind that Mary's *fiat* had to be included in the Annunciation phrases. This event and her reaction to it established her role as the "new Eve." Her freely willed obedience undid the disobedience of Eve in Genesis 3.

It is also worth noting that I was very deliberate in the order and choices made for the Nativity Mystery. My intention was to show how Jesus was announced to the poor, sought by the wise, and caused the worldly to be troubled. Then, my intention was to show the corresponding reactions, in parallel, – glory and praise, homage and gifts, and attempted murder, respectively. I submit that the reactions of these particular groups remain as relevant today as they were at the time of Christ's birth.

---

[25] St. Justin Martyr, *Dialogue with Trypho*, ca 155-160 AD, Chapter 78, from http://www.earlychristianwritings.com/text/justinmartyr-dialoguetrypho.html

Chapter 4: Bases for the Phrases Chosen

SORROWFUL MYSTERIES

I have taken the most elements from outside of Sacred Scripture in the phrases for The Sorrowful Mysteries. This was necessitated by the fact that many elements of the Scourging, Crowning with Thorns, and Carrying of the Cross are not contained within the Scriptures.

That said, the entire content of The Agony in the Garden, and all but one element of The Crucifixion and Death of Jesus were taken directly from Sacred Scripture.

The Second Sorrowful Mystery

I began the phrases for the Mystery of the Scourging at the Pillar before the scourging began. The first Phrase is "…who was blindfolded and beaten by the Temple guards." I felt that this beating by the Temple guards was the beginning of the physical torture of Jesus and an important event that links together the Agony in the Garden and the Scourging.

The details surrounding the Scourging at the Pillar are completely missing in Scripture and the only thing said about it in all four Gospels, paraphrasing, was 'and [Pilate] had Jesus scourged.' Obviously, that leaves much information out. To make up for this paucity of information, I searched for historical information about Roman scourging practices. I was delighted to find that the medical aspects of scourging have been the subject of several papers in reputable journals. I made use of three papers in particular, all by medical doctors. [26,27,28] At least one of whom based his findings on a study of detailed photographs of the Shroud of Turin. The phrases for beads three through eight are based on these medical journal articles.

The phrases for beads 6, 7, and 8 are quite graphic, but in my mind are necessarily so, to help us remember that Jesus was not just roughed up by the Romans, he was brutally beaten. Given enough time, He probably could have died from the blood loss of the scourging alone. This is why He died after only three hours on the Cross and did not have to have his legs broken as the criminals on either side of Him did.

The phrases for the final two beads are based on Isaiah's Suffering Servant prophecy and Peter's interpretation of that prophecy given in his first letter, second chapter. I believe that they will help the person praying the Rosary to remember why Jesus endured this suffering, which is important in eliciting a response from us.

The Third Sorrowful Mystery

The first two phrases for the third Sorrowful Mystery, the Crowning with Thorns, are based on Sacred Scripture. The third

---

[26] C. Truman Davis, MD, The Passion of Christ from a Medical Point of View, Arizona Medicine, 1965

[27] Wlliam D. Edwards, MD, Wesley, J. Gabel, and Floyd S. Hosmer, On the Physical Death of Jesus Christ, J Am Med Assoc 255(11), 1986

[28] Robert Bucklin, MD, The Medical Aspects of the Crucifixion of Our Lord Jesus Christ, Linacre Quarterly 25(1), Article 13, 1958

Chapter 4: Bases for the Phrases Chosen

and fifth phrases are based on the article by Bucklin from analysis of the Shroud of Turin.[29] The fourth phrase is based on a book written by "A Passionist Father" on the Mystery of the Crown of Thorns. In this book, the Father states that when the Roman soldiers pressed the crown onto Jesus' head, the sharp thorns "…pierce the skin, penetrate the skull, and prick the very brain of our dear Lord." Given that it is very difficult to ascertain whether the skull was actually pierced, I have reduced the severity to something that would be certain. The thorns would clearly have pierced the scalp. Beneath the scalp are several layers of soft tissues (skin, epicranial aponeurosis, and the pericranium with some connective tissue in between). These soft tissues would likely be penetrated by the sharp rigid thorns. While they may not break through the skull, they would likely get through the soft tissues including the periosteum (pericranium) which is a thin, tough membrane adhering to the outer surface of nearly all bones.[30] This would likely be torn by the sharp point of a thorn. Hence, the phrase, "…whose holy skull was scratched."

The phrase for the eighth bead is drawn from Isaiah chapter 50 verse 6. While none of the Gospels actually say this, it was one of the events in the life of the Suffering Servant prophesied by Isaiah, and so included. It is not unreasonable to assume this did happen to Jesus since the plucking of another man's beard in Jesus' time was considered a serious insult (see 2 Samuel 10:4), and that was

---

[29] Ibid.

[30] Stephen W. Rouhana, "Fluid Flow and Mechanical Damping in Bovine Cortical Bone," PhD diss, Rensselaer Polytechnic Institute, 1983

certainly the goal of the Roman soldiers during the scourging and crucifixion.

The Fourth Sorrowful Mystery

Again, Scripture is somewhat lacking in details for the Way of the Cross. Therefore, to fill in the details, I have chosen to use phrases taken from a meditation on the Stations of the Cross by St. Pope John Paul II.[31]

The Fifth Sorrowful Mystery

The Crucifixion and Death of Jesus are described in great detail and so most of the phrases for this mystery are directly adapted from Sacred Scripture.

Of significance, in this most grave Mystery, is that I have incorporated the seven last words of Christ as set forth in Fulton Sheen's classic work "Life of Christ."[32] These phrases occupy beads three through nine of the decade.

However, I began this Mystery with the phrase "…whose clothes were stripped from Him" to emphasize the intentional humiliation of Jesus by the Romans. This was part of crucifixion, and I believe it would benefit all of us to remember how low our God condescended to save us. This should be in the forefront of our minds as we pray the last Mystery.

---

[31] St. Pope John Paul II, Stations of the Cross Meditation and Prayers, 4/21/2000

[32] Fulton J. Sheen, *Life of Christ*, McGraw-Hill, New York, 1958.

The first part of the phrase for the fifth bead "…who said 'Woman, behold your son'" comes from John's Gospel. The second part "when He gave you to the Church as our Mother" comes from a Traditional understanding that when Jesus said "behold thy son" to Mary at the foot of the Cross, and when he said to St. John, "behold thy mother," implicit in these words was his gift of the Church to Mary and of Mary to all Christians as we became her adopted children. Mary's title of "Mother of the Church" is ancient and has been found in the works of St. Ambrose as referenced by St. Pope John Paul II.[33] It was also used by the Congregation of Divine Worship and the Discipline of Sacraments when, in 2018, they issued the Decree on the celebration of the Blessed Virgin Mary Mother of the Church.[34]

LUMINOUS MYSTERIES

The First Luminous Mystery

The phrases for the first Luminous Mystery are taken entirely from Sacred Scripture. As in the Glorious Mysteries, I have blended St. John's account of the Baptism of Jesus with that of another account; in this case, that of the Synoptic Gospels. Again, I find no contradiction and have taken phrases that highlight John the Baptist's self-awareness that he is just the messenger.

---

[33] St. Pope John Paul II, *Redemptoris Mater*, No. 25, Para. 2, 3/25/1987

[34] Congregation of Divine Worship and the Discipline of the Sacraments, *Decree on the celebration of the Blessed Virgin Mary Mother of the Church in the General Roman Calendar*, 2/11/2018

The Second Luminous Mystery

The phrases for the Wedding Feast at Cana are all from St. John's Gospel. However, I was struck with a new insight as I read this account searching for the right phrases to use. For the first time in my life, I noticed that John referred to the wedding taking place on the third day after the Baptism of Jesus. Given that this was the first recorded miracle of Jesus, one could say that Jesus manifested His glory to the Apostles in the form of His mastery of material nature during this event. I felt that the parallelism with the manifestation of His glory in the Resurrection on the third day, deserved to be noticed. Therefore, I began the Second Luminous Mystery with the fact that it was the third day, and closed the Mystery with the fact that Jesus manifested His glory to the Apostles on the third day to draw that parallel to the mind of the person praying the Rosary.

The Third, Fourth, and Fifth Mysteries

The phrases chosen for these Mysteries are all derived from Sacred Scripture with the exception of the phrases for the second and third beads of the Fifth Luminous Mystery, The Gift of the Eucharist. For those two beads, I have chosen to use the Words of Institution from Eucharistic Prayers I-IV in the 3rd Edition of the Roman Missal. [35] For the average church-going Catholic, these

---

[35] International Committee on English in the Liturgy, Inc., *Excerpts from the English translation of The Roman Missal,* 2011

words are much more familiar than the actual words used in the various translations in Sacred Scripture. Therefore, I believe they will be more memorable than the actual text from Scripture. Since the Church has chosen to use these words in the Sacred Liturgy, I did not hesitate to use them here.

For the mystery of the Gift of the Eucharist, I intentionally chose phrases that were direct quotes of Jesus that prove His intention is that the Eucharist is not just a symbol, but is His Real Presence, that is, His Body, Blood, Soul, and Divinity.

CHAPTER 5

SOME QUESTIONS AND ANSWERS ABOUT THIS METHOD

Is this method of praying the Rosary sacrilegious? The Rosary has been around for centuries. Mary herself told the children of Fatima to pray it. How can we make changes to it?

I answer that, if there are those who do not pray the Rosary because they cannot focus, or because they become bored by the repetition, this method may help bring them back or help them start, because they cannot help but focus on the life of Christ when praying the phrases and each one is different. The basic prayers of the Rosary remain unchanged, and the person praying it contemplates more explicitly the lives of Jesus and Mary. Therefore, the basic Rosary is unchanged but made richer by the addition of material that elicits the Christian Mystery as called for by St. Pope John Paul. As a bonus, if this adds to the number of people praying the Rosary, that is a very good outcome.

Is this method of praying the Rosary for everyone?

I answer that, just as there are many patron saints to whom we appeal for intercession, and just as there are many canons by which the Eucharist is consecrated, so there can be many efficacious ways of praying the Rosary, even for the same person, depending on mood or circumstance. Perhaps my training as a scientist prevents me from entering deeply into contemplation since my mind is very active and I have great trouble shutting it down. But, I have found that this Structured Contemplative Rosary, although not perfect by any means, works wonders for helping me stay focused on Jesus through Mary.

However, if the prayer phrases haven't been memorized, it would be very difficult to pray this Rosary while driving or walking somewhere without the Charts. In such cases, one could opt to pray the Rosary in the traditional way. Or still, when time is short, but one really wants to pray a quick Rosary, one might use the traditional method.

<u>Does this method take away any hope for contemplation while praying the Rosary?</u>

I answer that, our personal prayer life, in contrast with our communal prayer life, is a very individual thing. We all relate to our Lord and His Mother in our own ways. Some people use the Rosary as a contemplative method where the prayers are the background for opening up their minds and hearts to Jesus. They can still do so. Others, are entirely able to focus on our Lord while praying the standard Rosary. Such people may have no need or desire to use this more prescriptive approach.

Chapter 5: Some Questions and Answers about this Method

<u>Can this method be used in a public recitation of the Rosary?</u>

I answer that, in a public setting, such as a visitation at a funeral parlor, where most people would be unfamiliar with the Meditative Rosary, one may want to pray the Rosary in a traditional way. **However**, since the leader always says the Hail Mary prayer in a public recitation of the Rosary, it won't matter that the other people don't know the phrases, because the leader is the only one to say them. So, as long as the leader has the Phrase Charts, or has memorized the phrases, this method can be used.

Caveat Emptor: I would suggest giving the participants in prayer some advisement that a different method of praying will be used, and giving them an example so that they are not caught by surprise. I once tried to use this method at a home for the elderly where I do a monthly Communion Service, and it fell flat on its face. I had not given them enough information, and they seemed to be confused by the new method.

CHAPTER 6

CONCLUSION

It may be difficult at first to pray the Rosary using the Structured Contemplative Method without the Phrase Charts. It will be nearly impossible to do while doing other things. **Please do not use the Phrase Charts while driving!** It's one thing to pray the Rosary from memory while driving and quite a different thing to be reading the phrases.

With some time, you may be surprised at the fact that you can recall all of the phrases, especially if you pray the Rosary daily. It really isn't necessary to be concerned about whether the words you remember are exactly right. These phrases are mainly to give some structure to the contemplation so that the events in Jesus' life can be recalled as you pray the Rosary. In fact, even if you reorder the words, it does not usually change the meaning. For example, in the Nativity of the Lord, within the Joyful Mysteries, you might say "…with whom you were pregnant when you traveled <u>to Bethlehem with Joseph</u> for the census" instead of "…with whom you were pregnant when you traveled <u>with Joseph to Bethlehem</u> for the census." Clearly, the meaning is not changed. So, one might think of the phrases as being "forgiving." They can be used a guide to the meditation that gives it some structure without being a slave to them. Remember what Saint Pope John Paul II said in his Apostolic Letter, the method is "a means to an end and cannot become an end in itself." The "end" is to use the Rosary to contemplate, and connect with, the life of Jesus and Mary.

In an effort to help you appreciate the flow of the Rosary using this method, I've recorded a short introduction and all of the mysteries for you to pray along with. The QR code at the end of this book, mentioned earlier, will take you to the website housing the recordings.

May God Bless your efforts, and may St. Louis de Montford, intercede for you as you pray every one of your Holy Rosaries!!

CHAPTER 7

PHRASE CHARTS AND REFERENCE/CITATION CHARTS

The Glorious Mysteries

Phrase Chart for

The Resurrection
…whose body was laid to rest on Good Friday in a new tomb by Joseph of Arimathea
…whose tomb was guarded by Pilate's order
…whose body Mary Magdalene went to anoint early on Sunday morning
…whose tombstone was rolled away when Mary arrived
…whose body was not in the tomb
…who two Angels said had been raised from the dead
…who appeared to Mary Magdalene as she turned to go tell the other disciples
…whose burial cloths were found in the tomb by Peter and John
…who appeared to you and the other disciples in the upper room
…who appeared to the disciples on the road to Emmaus

The Glorious Mysteries

Reference Chart for

The Resurrection
Mt: 27:57-60; Mk 15:42-46; Lk 23:50-53; Jn 19:38-42
Mt 27:62-66
Mt 28:1; Mk 16:1; Lk 24:1-10; Jn 20:1
Mt 28:2; Mk 16:4; Lk 24:2; Jn 20:1
Mt 28:6; Mk 16:6; Lk 24:3; Jn 20:2-10
Mt 28:6; Mk 16:6; Lk 24:5
Mt 28:9; Jn 20:15-18
Lk 24:12; Jn 20:5-7
Mk 16:14; Lk 24:36; Jn 20:19-28
Mk 16:12; Lk 24:13-35

The Glorious Mysteries

Phrase Chart for

The Ascension
...who led the disciples out from Jerusalem to the Mount of Olives
...whom the disciples asked if He would now restore the Kingdom to Israel
...who said it is not for us to know the times and seasons the Father has established by His own authority
...who said "Go therefore and make disciples of all nations, baptizing them in the name of the Father, and of the Son, and of the Holy Spirit, teaching them to observe all that I have commanded you."
...who was lifted up in front of the disciples
...who disappeared into a cloud
...who two angels said had been taken up into Heaven
...who the angels said would return the same way that He had gone into Heaven
...whom the disciples worshipped before returning to Jerusalem with great joy
...who is seated at the right hand of the Father

The Glorious Mysteries

Reference Chart for

The Ascension
Lk 24:50; Acts 1:12
Acts 1:6
Acts 1:7
Mt 28:19-20
Mk 16:19; Lk 24:51; Acts 1:9
Acts 1:9
Acts 1:10-11
Acts 1:11
Lk 24:52
Mk 16:19

The Glorious Mysteries

Phrase Chart for

The Gift of the Holy Spirit
...who told the disciples to wait in Jerusalem for the "Promise of the Father"
...who appeared to you and the disciples in the upper room even though the door was locked
...who said "Peace be with you"
...who said "As the Father has sent me, so I send you"
...who breathed on the disciples
...who said "Receive the Holy Spirit"
...who said "Whose sins you forgive are forgiven them, and whose sins you retain are retained"
...who sent the Spirit with a noise from the sky like "a strong driving wind"
...who sent the Spirit as "tongues of fire," which came to rest on each of the disciples
...whose Spirit allowed the disciples to boldly proclaim the Gospel in many different tongues

The Glorious Mysteries

Reference Chart for

The Gift of the Holy Spirit
Lk 24:49; Acts 1:4-5
Lk 24:36; Mk 16:14; Jn 20:19-29
Lk 24:36; Jn 20:19, 21, 26
Jn 20:21
Jn 20:22
Jn 20:22
Jn 20:23
Acts 2:2
Acts 2:3
Acts 2:4

The Glorious Mysteries

Phrase Chart for

The Assumption of Mary into Heaven
…whose foreseen merits allowed you to be conceived without Original Sin
…whom you consented to bear into the world
…for whom you were Theotokos, God-bearer, Mother of God
…for whom you were the Ark of the New Covenant
…whom you conceived, brought forth, and nourished
…for whom you fulfilled all the prescriptions of the law
…of whose you were the first disciple
…whom you accompanied through His whole life, Passion, and death
…who refused to allow your body to experience the corruption of death
…who took you up into Heaven at the end of your life on earth

The Glorious Mysteries

Reference Chart for

The Assumption of Mary into Heaven
Ineffabilis Deus (1854); *Constitution Cum Praeexcelsa* of Sixtus IV (1477) from Neuner and Depuis #704*; Council of Trent (1546) from Neuner & Depuis # 705
Lk 1:38
Lk 1:43; Council of Ephesus (431)
Munificentissimus Deus [34] (1950); *Ineffabilis Deus* – [Para 24] (1854)
Lumen Gentium [61] (1964)
Lk 2:39
Redemptoris Mater [26 Para 5, 12,13,17,20] (1987); *Lumen Gentium* [58] (1964)
Jn 19:25
Munificentissimus Deus [32, 35] (1950);
Munificentissimus Deus [25] (1950);

* J. Neuner and J. Depuis, *The Christian Faith in the Doctrinal Documents of the Catholic Church*, 2001.

The Glorious Mysteries

Phrase Chart for

The Crowning of Mary, Queen of Heaven & Earth
...who crowned you, Mary, Queen of Heaven and Earth
...who crowned you, Mary, Queen of Angels
...who crowned you, Mary, Queen of the Apostles
...who crowned you, Mary, Queen of Martyrs
...who crowned you, Mary, Queen of the Patriarchs
...who crowned you, Mary, Queen of all Saints
...who crowned you, Mary, Queen of Peace*
...who crowned you, Mary, Queen Conceived without Original Sin
...who crowned you, Mary, Queen Assumed into Heaven
...who crowned you, Mary, Queen of the Most Holy Rosary

*For particular devotions the following, or similar, may be substituted: ...who crowned you, Our Lady of Good Counsel, Our Lady of Czestochowa, Our Lady of Fatima, Our Lady of Lourdes, Our Lady of Guadeloupe, Our Lady of Grace.

The Glorious Mysteries

Reference Chart for

The Crowning of Mary, Queen of Heaven & Earth
Munificentissimus Deus [26, 28] (1950);
Litany of Loreto (P. Sixtus V, 1587)
Litany of Loreto (P. Sixtus V, 1587)
Litany of Loreto (P. Sixtus V, 1587)
Litany of Loreto (P. Sixtus V, 1587)
Litany of Loreto (P. Sixtus V, 1587)
Litany of Loreto (P. Sixtus V, 1587, title added in 1917 by Pope Benedict XV)
Litany of Loreto (P. Sixtus V, 1587, title added in 1883 by Pope Leo XIII for the whole Church)
Litany of Loreto (P. Sixtus V, 1587, title added in 1950 by Pope Pius XII)
Litany of Loreto (P. Sixtus V, 1587, title added in 1675 for the confraternities of the Holy Rosary)

The Joyful Mysteries

Phrase Chart for

The Annunciation
…for whom the Father sent the angel Gabriel to you
…whom Gabriel asked you to bear into the world
…who, Gabriel said, would be called the Son of the Most High
…who, Gabriel said, would be called holy
…who, Gabriel said, would sit on the throne of David His father
…who, Gabriel said, would rule over the house of Jacob forever
…whose kingdom, Gabriel said, would never end
…who would become the adopted son of Joseph of the house of David
…whom you agreed to bear when you said "Behold I am the handmaid of the Lord. May it be done to me according to your word."
…whom you conceived through the Holy Spirit by the power of the Most High

The Joyful Mysteries

Reference Chart for

The Annunciation
Lk 1:26
Lk 1:31
Lk 1:32
Lk 1:35
Lk 1:32
Lk 1:33
Lk 1:33
Lk 1:27
Lk 1:38
Lk 1:35

The Joyful Mysteries

Phrase Chart for

The Visitation
…with whom you were pregnant when you traveled to the house of Zechariah in the hill country of Judah
…with whom you were pregnant when visited your cousin Elizabeth there
…whose cousin John the Baptist was in Elizabeth's womb
…whose presence caused the infant John to leap for joy
…in appreciation for whom Elizabeth cried out "Most blessed are you among women and blessed is the fruit of your womb."
…in appreciation for whom Elizabeth said "And how is it that the mother of my Lord comes to me?
… in appreciation for whom you said "My soul proclaims the greatness of the Lord, and my spirit rejoices in God my savior"
…in thanksgiving for whom you said "The Mighty One has done great things for me and holy is His name"
…in thanksgiving for whom you said "His mercy is from age to age to those who fear Him"
… with whom you were pregnant while you remained with Elizabeth for three months

The Joyful Mysteries

Reference Chart for

The Visitation
Lk 1:39-40
Lk 1:40
Lk 1:41
Lk 1:41
Lk 1:42
Lk 1:43
Lk 1:46
Lk 1:49
Lk 1:50
Lk 1:56

The Joyful Mysteries

Phrase Chart for

The Nativity
…with whom you were pregnant when you traveled with Joseph to Bethlehem for the census
…for whom there was no room at the inn
…who was born in a cave
…who had a manger for his crib
…whose birth was announced to the shepherds
…for whom the wise men from the east searched
…about whom Herod was greatly troubled
…for whom the shepherds glorified and praised God
…to whom the magi paid homage and brought gifts of gold, frankincense, and myrrh
…whom Joseph took with you to Egypt to escape Herod's Massacre of the Innocents

The Joyful Mysteries

Reference Chart for

The Nativity
Lk 2:1-5
Lk 2:7
St, Justin Martyr - Dialogue with Trypho [78] (150)
Lk 2:7
Lk 2:8-14
Mt 2:1-9
Mt 2:3
Lk 2:15-20
Mt 2:11
Mt 2:13-18

The Joyful Mysteries

Phrase Chart for

The Presentation in the Temple
...who was circumcised on the eighth day after birth
...whom you took with you to Jerusalem for your ritual purification
...whom you presented to the Lord in the Temple according to the law of Moses
...for whom you offered the prescribed sacrifice
...about whom Simeon said "Now, Master, you may let your servant go in peace according to your word for my eyes have seen your salvation."
...about whom Simeon said He will be "a light for revelation to the Gentiles...."
...about whom Simeon said to you, "Behold, this child is destined for the fall and rise of many in Israel and to be a sign that will be contradicted and you yourself a sword will pierce"
...for whom Anna the prophetess also gave thanks to God
...for whom you fulfilled all the prescriptions of the law before returning to Nazareth
...who grew in wisdom, and upon whom the favor of the Father rested

The Joyful Mysteries

Reference Chart for

The Presentation in the Temple
Lk 2:21
Lk 2:22
Lk 2:22-23
Lk 2:24
Lk 2:25-30
Lk 2:32
Lk 2:34-35
Lk 2:36-38
Lk 2:39
Lk 2:40

The Joyful Mysteries

Phrase Chart for

The Finding in the Temple
…who went up with you to Jerusalem for the Passover when he was twelve years old
…who stayed behind in Jerusalem without your knowledge when your caravan left
…whom you could not find in your caravan after the first day of travel
…for whom you returned to Jerusalem
…for whom you searched for three days
…whom you found in the Temple sitting in the midst of the teachers, listening to them and asking them questions
…who amazed all who heard Him by His understanding and answers
…to whom you said "Son why have you done this to us? Your father and I have been looking for you with great anxiety"
…who said "Why were you looking for me? Did you not know that I must be in my Father's house?
…who went down with you to Nazareth and was obedient to you

The Joyful Mysteries

Reference Chart for

The Finding in the Temple
Lk 2:41-42
Lk 2:43
Lk 2:44
Lk 2:45
Lk 2:46
Lk 2:46
Lk 2:47
Lk 2:48
Lk 2:49
Lk 2:51

The Sorrowful Mysteries

Phrase Chart for

The Agony in the Garden
...who after eating the Last Supper, took His disciples across the Kidron Valley to the Garden of Gethsemane to pray
...who to told the disciples to stay alert and pray that they not be put to the test
...who went off by Himself to pray
...who asked the Father to take His cup of suffering away
...who said to the Father, "not my will but Yours be done"
...who returned three times to find His disciples sleeping
...who said to them "So you could not keep watch with me for one hour?" and then, went off by Himself again to pray
...who prayed so intently that "His sweat became like drops of blood"
...who saw the Temple guards approaching
...who was betrayed by a kiss

The Sorrowful Mysteries

Reference Chart for

The Agony in the Garden
Mt 26:36; Mk 14:32; Lk 22:40; Jn 18:1
Mt 26:36; Mk 14:32; Lk 22:40
Mt 26:39; Mk 14:35; Lk 22:41
Mt 26:39; Mk 14:36; Lk 22:42
Mt 26:39; Mk 14:36; Lk 22:42
Mt 26:40; Mk 14:37; Lk 22:45
Mt 26:40-42; Mk 14:37-39; Lk 22:45-46
Lk 22:44
Mt 26:47; Mk 14:43; Lk 22:47; Jn 18:3-4
Mt 26:48; Mk 14:44; Lk 22:48

The Sorrowful Mysteries

Phrase Chart for

The Scourging at the Pillar
…who was blindfolded and beaten by the Temple guards
…who was condemned by Pontius Pilate to be scourged
…who had His clothes stripped from Him
…who was tied to a pillar
…who was whipped with the flagrum
…whose sacred skin was slashed
…whose holy muscles and sinews were torn
…whose precious blood was spilled
…who was pierced for our transgressions
…by whose stripes we are healed

The Sorrowful Mysteries

Reference Chart for

The Scourging at the Pillar
Mt 26:67; Mk14:65; Lk 22:63
Mt 27:26; Mk 15:15; Jn 19:1
Davis, 1965; Edwards et al. 1986
Davis, 1965; Edwards et al. 1986
Davis, 1965; Edwards et al. 1986
Davis, 1965; Edwards et al. 1986
Davis, 1965; Edwards et al. 1986
Davis, 1965; Edwards et al. 1986
Isaiah 53:5
Isaiah 53:5; 1 Pet 2:24

C. Truman Davis, MD, *The Passion of Christ from a Medical Point of View*, Arizona Medicine, 1965.

William D. Edwards, MD, Wesley, J. Gabel, and Floyd S. Hosmer, *On the Physical Death of Jesus Christ*, J Am Med Assoc 255(11), 1986.

The Sorrowful Mysteries

Phrase Chart for

The Crowning with Thorns
...for whom they wove a crown of thorns
...upon whose head they pressed the crown
...whose sacred scalp was pierced
...whose holy skull was scratched
...whose precious blood was spilled
...on whose injured shoulders they placed a purple robe
...in whose hand they placed a reed as a mock scepter
...whose beard they plucked
...in whose face they spat
...whom they mocked as king of the Jews

Robert Bucklin, MD, *The Medical Aspects of the Crucifixion of Our Lord Jesus Christ*, Linacre Quarterly 25(1), Article 13, 1958.

C. Truman Davis, MD, *The Passion of Christ from a Medical Point of View*, Arizona Medicine, 1965.

William D. Edwards, MD, Wesley, J. Gabel, and Floyd S. Hosmer, *On the Physical Death of Jesus Christ*, J Am Med Assoc 255(11), 1986.

The Sorrowful Mysteries

Reference Chart for

The Crowning with Thorns
Mt 27:29; Mk 15:17; Jn 19:2
Mt 27:29; Mk 15:17; Jn 19:2
Bucklin, 1958
A Passionist Father, 1999
Bucklin, 1958
Mt 27:28; Mk 15:17; Jn 19:2
Mt 27:29; Jn 19:2
Isaiah 50:6
Mt 27:30; Mk 15:19; Isaiah 50:6
Mt 27:29; Mk 15:18; Jn 19:3

A Passionist Father, *The Mystery of the Crown of Thorns*, Preserving Christian Publications, Inc., New York, 1999, pg. 60.

Stephen W. Rouhana, PhD *Fluid Flow and Mechanical Damping in Bovine Cortical Bone*, PhD dissertation, Rensselaer Polytechnic Institute, 1983.

The Sorrowful Mysteries

Phrase Chart for

The Carrying of the Cross
…upon whose shoulders they placed the crossbeam
…who fell the first time
…who saw you, His mother
…for whom they enlisted Simon of Cyrene to help carry the cross
…whose face was wiped by Veronica and who left His image on her veil
…who fell the second time
…who saw the women of Jerusalem
…who told the women to mourn for themselves and for their children and not for Him
…who fell the third time
…who carried the cross to Calvary

The Sorrowful Mysteries

Reference Chart for

The Carrying of the Cross
Jn 19:16-17
Stations of the Cross Meditation and Prayers by St. Pope John Paul II, 4/21/2000
Stations of the Cross Meditation and Prayers by St. Pope John Paul II, 4/21/2000
Mt 27:32; Mk 15:21; Lk 23:26
Stations of the Cross Meditation and Prayers by St. Pope John Paul II, 4/21/2000
Stations of the Cross Meditation and Prayers by St. Pope John Paul II, 4/21/2000
Lk 23:28
Lk 23:28
Stations of the Cross Meditation and Prayers by St. Pope John Paul II, 4/21/2000
Mt 27:33; Mk 15:22; Lk 23:33; Jn 19:17

The Sorrowful Mysteries

Phrase Chart for

The Crucifixion and Death of Jesus
…whose clothes were stripped from Him
…whose hands and feet were nailed to the cross
…who was lifted high above the earth on the wood of the cross and said "Father, forgive them, for they know not what they do"
…who said to the good thief, "I promise you, this day you will be with Me in paradise"
…who said "Woman, behold your son" when He gave you to the Church as our Mother
…who said *"Eli, Eli, lema sebachtani"* "My God, my God, why have you forsaken me?"
…who said, "I Thirst" meaning that He thirsts for all souls to come to Heaven
…who said "It is finished"
…who cried out in a loud voice and said "Father into Your hands I commend my Spirit"
…who, although He had died, had a lance thrust into His heart, and from the wound, blood and water flowed, showing His Divine Love and Divine Mercy

The Sorrowful Mysteries

Reference Chart for

The Crucifixion and Death of Jesus
Mt 27:35; Mk 15:24; Lk 23:34; Jn 19:23-24
Mt 27:35; Mk 15:24; Lk 23:33; Jn 19:18
Jn 8:28; Jn 12:32; Lk 23:34
Lk 24:43
Jn 19:26-27; Since St. Ambrose in the 4th Century, Mary has been called "Mother of the Church"; See von Balthasar and Ratzinger below; See also *Redemptoris Mater* No 1, Para 3, Footnote 3 and Sect 42, Para 3, Footnote 120
Mt 27:46; Mk 15:34
Jn 19:28; St. Teresa of Calcutta Reflection on "I Thirst" Darjeeling, Sept. 10, 1946; CCC 74
Jn 19:30 ("It is finished")
Mt 27:50; Mk 15:37; Lk 23:46 (Cried out…); Jn 19:30
Jn 19:33-34; St. Faustina Kowalska Diary Entries 299, 1074

Hans Urs von Balthasar and Joseph Cardinal Raztinger, *Mary the Church at the Source*, Ignatius Press, San Francisco, 2005, pg 141.

The Luminous Mysteries

Phrase Chart for

The Baptism in the Jordan
…about whom John the Baptist said "Prepare the way of the Lord"
…about whom John said "I am not worthy to untie His sandals"
…about whom John said He will baptize with the Holy Spirit and fire
…about whom John said "Behold the Lamb of God"
…about whom John said He "takes away the sin of the world"
…to whom John said "I need to baptized by you, yet you come to me?"
…who said "Let it be so…to fulfill all righteousness"
…who was baptized in the Jordan River
…upon whom the Holy Spirit descended like a dove
…about whom a voice from Heaven said "This is my beloved Son, in whom I am well pleased"

The Luminous Mysteries

Reference Chart for

The Baptism in the Jordan
Mt 3:3; Mk1:3; Lk 3:4; Jn 1:23
Mt 3:11; Mk 1:7; Lk 3:16; Jn 1:26
Mt 3:11; Mk 1:8; Lk 3:16; Jn 1:33
Jn 1:29; Jn 1:36
Jn 1:29
Mt 3:14
Mt 3:15
Mt 3:16; Mk 1:9; Lk 3:21
Mt 3:16; Mk 1:10; Lk 3:22; Jn 1:32
Mt 3:17; Mk 1:11; Lk 3:22

The Luminous Mysteries

Phrase Chart for

The Wedding Feast at Cana
…who "on the third day" after His baptism was in Cana of Galilee
…who was invited with you and His disciples to a wedding feast
…to whom you said "They have no wine"
…who said to you "Woman, how does your concern affect me?"
…who said to you "My hour has not yet come"
…about whom you said to the servers to "Do whatever He tells you"
…who saw six stone water jars
…who told the servers to fill the jars with water
…who changed the water into wine
…who on the third day, manifested His glory to His disciples

The Luminous Mysteries

Reference Chart for

The Wedding Feast at Cana
Jn 2:1
Jn 2:2
Jn 2:3
Jn 2:4
Jn 2:4
Jn 2:5
Jn 2:6
Jn 2:7
Jn 2:8
Jn 2:11

The Luminous Mysteries

Phrase Chart for

The Preaching of the Kingdom of God
…who went to the synagogue in Nazareth
…who was handed the scroll of the Prophet Isaiah
…who read out loud "The Spirit of the Lord is upon me because He has anointed me to bring glad tidings to the poor…"
…who said "Today this scripture passage is fulfilled in your hearing"
…who was sent to proclaim the good news of the Kingdom
…who restored sight to the blind
…who released those held captive by Satan
…who raised the dead
…who gave us the Beatitudes
…who taught us how to pray with the Lord's Prayer

The Luminous Mysteries

Reference Chart for

The Preaching of the Kingdom of God
Mt 13:54; Mk 6:1; Lk 4:16
Lk 4:17
Lk 4:18
Lk 4:21
Mt 4:23; Mk 1:38-39; Lk 4:43-44; Mt 9:35; Mt 10:7; Lk 9:2; Mt 11:4; Lk 7:22; Lk 16:16; Mt 11:28; Lk 8:1; Mt 12:28; Lk 17:20
Blind Mt 9:27; Mk 8:22; Mt 20:29-34; Mk 10:46-52; Lk 18:35-43; Jn 9:1-7
Release Mt 8:16; Mk 1:34; Lk4:41; Mt 8:28; Mt 9:32; Mt. 12:22; Mk 3:22; Lk 11:14
Lk 7:11-17; Mt 9:18-26; Mk 5:21-43; Lk 8:40-56; Jn 11:1-44
Mt 5:1-12; Lk 6:20-23
Mt 6:9-15; Lk 11:2-4

The Luminous Mysteries

Phrase Chart for

The Transfiguration
…who took Peter, James, and John up a high mountain to pray
…who was transfigured before them
…whose face shone like the sun
…whose clothes became dazzling white
…with whom Moses and Elijah appeared in glory
…who spoke with them about His imminent departure from Jerusalem
…to whom Peter said "it is good for us to be here"
…who was overshadowed by a cloud
…about whom a voice from the cloud said "This is my beloved Son, listen to Him"
…who told the apostles not to tell anyone about the vision until He had been raised from the dead

The Luminous Mysteries

Reference Chart for

The Transfiguration
Mt 17:1; Mk 9:2; Lk 9:28
Mt 17:2; Mk 9:2; Lk 9:29
Mt 17:2; Lk 9:29
Mt 17:2; Mk 9:3; Lk 9:29
Mt 17:3; Mk 9:4; Lk 9:30
Mt 17:3; Mk 9:4; Lk 9:31
Mt 17:4; Mk 9:5; Lk 9:33
Mt 17:5; Mk 9:7; Lk 9:34
Mt 17:5; Mk 9:7; Lk 9:35
Mt 17:9; Mk 9:9

The Luminous Mysteries

Phrase Chart for

The Gift of the Eucharist
…who greatly desired to eat the Passover supper with His disciples
…who while they were at supper, took the bread, blessed it, broke it, and gave it to them saying "Take this all of you and eat of it; for this is my body which will be given up for you"
…who likewise took the cup and said "Take this all of you and drink from it; for this is the chalice of my blood, the blood of the new and eternal covenant, which will be poured out for you and for many, for the forgiveness of sins. Do this in memory of me."
…who said "Unless you eat the flesh of the Son of Man and drink His blood, you do not have life within you"
…who said "For my flesh is true food"
…who said "and my blood is true drink"
…who said "Whoever eats my flesh and drinks my blood, has eternal life and I will raise him on the last day."
…the true manna come down from Heaven
…the Bread of Life
…who is truly present, Body, Blood, Soul, and Divinity in the Eucharist

The Luminous Mysteries

Reference Chart for

The Gift of the Eucharist
Lk 22:15
The Words of Institution from Eucharistic Prayers I-IV in the 3rd Edition of the Roman Missal, 2011
The Words of Institution from Eucharistic Prayers I-IV in the 3rd Edition of the Roman Missal, 2011
Jn 6:53
Jn 6:55
Jn 6:55
Jn 6:54
Jn 6:32, 51
Jn 6:35, 48
CCC 1374; Council of Trent in 1551

APPENDIX

PORTABLE COMPREHENSIVE PHRASE CHARTS

Available for free download at
https://enroutebooksandmedia.com/contemplativerosary/

You Knew

Stephen W. Rouhana February 23, 2018

Every bruise of the fist, Every choke of the chain,
That was only the start of a time full of pain…

You knew.

Every lie to be told, Every false accusation,
The total rejection of the Israelite nation…

You knew.

Every slap on the cheek, Every spit in the face,
The unbearable sin of the whole human race…

You knew.

Every welt of the rod, Every tear of the whip,
Every inch of your skin, as it started to rip…

You knew.

Every poke of a thorn, Every scratch on Your skull,
Every moment of hope that the pain would get dull…

You knew.

Every pluck of the beard, Every taunt and derision, You could have said "No," it was all Your decision…

You knew.

The taunts of the crowd, their ridicule and laughter,
On your way to Golgotha and what would come after…

You knew.

The wound on your shoulder, The scrapes on Your knees,
The destination ahead to be nailed to the trees...

You knew.

That three times you would fall and impact the street,
The holes in Your hands, and The holes in Your feet…

You knew.

Every drop of Your blood, and the hole in Your Heart,
Your last human breath as You finished Your part...

You knew.

You knew all these things, before You ever said yes, yet,
You still went ahead.

YOU KNEW and YOU LOVED, so you still went ahead.

www.ingramcontent.com/pod-product-compliance
Lightning Source LLC
LaVergne TN
LVHW051845080426
835512LV00018B/3085